Read Write Inc.

Literacy and Language
Anthology

4

Janey Pursglove and **Charlotte Raby**

Series developed by **Ruth Miskin**

OXFORD

UNIVERSITY PRESS

OXFORD
UNIVERSITY PRESS

Great Clarendon Street, Oxford, OX2 6DP,
United Kingdom

Oxford University Press is a department of the
University of Oxford. It furthers the University's
objective of excellence in research, scholarship,
and education by publishing worldwide.
Oxford is a registered trade mark of Oxford University
Press in the UK and in certain other countries

British Library Cataloguing in Publication Data
Data available

ISBN: 978-0-19-833080-6

10 9 8 7 6 5 4 3 2 1

Paper used in the production of this book is a natural,
recyclable product made from wood grown in sustainable
forests. The manufacturing process conforms to the
environmental regulations of the country of origin.

Printed in China by Imago

Acknowledgements

Cover illustration by Chuck Groenink

Illustrations by: Leo Broadley; Neil Chapman; Lee Cosgrove;
Katie May Green; Chuck Groenink; Harriet Muncaster;
Lemniscates; Andrew Painter; Andres Martinez Ricci; Yannick
Robert; Ariel Sela; David Semple

The publishers would like to thank the following for the
permission to reproduce photographs: **p14** clockwise from
left: vasabii/Shutterstock; Pokomeda/Shutterstock; Yuriy
Kulyk/Shutterstock; AlamyCelebrity/Alamy; INTERFOTO/
Alamy; **p14-15**: silver tiger/Shutterstock; **p14-15**: MeiKIS/
Shutterstock; **p15tl**: 3alexd/iStock; **p15tr**: ZUMA Press, Inc./
Alamy; **p15b**: Colin Anderson/Getty Images; **p22-23**: Eka
Panova/Shutterstock; **p22-23**: diversepixel/Shutterstock;
p23: Steven Puetzer/Getty Images; **p39**: SoleilC/Shutterstock;
p50: scol22/iStock; **p51t**: Pablo Paul/Alamy; **p51m**: SuslO/
Shutterstock; **p51b**: 67photo/Alamy; **p53l**: TEK IMAGE/
SCIENCE PHOTO LIBRARY; **p53r**: ITV/Rex Features; **p65**:
Mary Evans/Peter Higginbotham Collection; **p66-67** Nataliia
Litovchenko/Shutterstock; **p65-66**: R-studio/Shutterstock;
p66t: nicoolay/iStock; **p66bl**: Antonio Abrignani/
Shutterstock; **p66br**: Mary Evans/Roger Worsley Archive;
p67: Morphart Creation/Shutterstock; **p78** clockwise
from top left: Peter Close/Shutterstock; Michelangelus/
Shutterstock; Kuzma/Shutterstock; Eric Isselee/Shutterstock;
p78-79: Seamartini Graphics/Shutterstock; **p79**: swinner/
Shutterstock; Ed Isaacs/Shutterstock

The authors and publisher are grateful to the following for
permission to reproduce copyright material:

Debjani Chatterjee p19 'My Sari', from *Masala: Poems from
India, Bangladesh and Sri Lanka* edited by Debjani Chatterjee
(Macmillan, 2005), copyright © Debjani Chatterjee 1999,
reprinted by permission of the author.

Wes Magee p20 'At the end of a School Day', published in
The Works 4 chosen by Pie Corbett & Gaby Morgan (Macmillan,
2005), copyright © Wes Magee 2005, reprinted by permission
of the author.

Kaye Umansky p26 *The Bogey Men and the Trolls Next Door*
(Dolphin, 1997), copyright © Kaye Umansky 1997, reprinted
by permission of the publishers, The Orion Publishing
Group, London.

We have made every effort to trace and contact all copyright
holders before publication. If notified, the publisher will rectify
any errors or omissions at the earliest opportunity.

The authors of the Fiction texts in this Anthology (excepting
those listed above) are as follows: **Narinder Dhami p4** *Lost
or Stolen?*, text © Oxford University Press 2013; **Lou Kuenzler
p40** *The Fly and the Fool*, text © Oxford University Press 2013;
Jim Eldridge p54 *Runaways!*, text © Oxford University Press
2013; **Pratima Mitchell p68** *Sugarcane Juice*, text © Oxford
University Press 2013

The authors of the Non-fiction texts in this Anthology are as
follows: **Adrian Bradbury p14** 'Gadget Magic'; **p16** 'The
Greatest Gadget of Them All'; **p22** 'Your Alien Experiences';
p24 'The Daily Blab', **p36** 'The Stellar Stage School'; **p38** 'How
the Voice Works'; **p50** 'Junior Detective'; **p64** 'London Herald'
© Oxford University Press 2013; **Charlotte Raby p78** 'VIPER!
– Critic's Review'; **p79** 'VIPER! – A Film Trailer © Oxford
University Press 2013

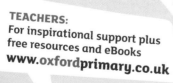

TEACHERS:
For inspirational support plus
free resources and eBooks
www.oxfordprimary.co.uk

PARENTS:
Help your child's learning
with essential tips, phonics
support and free eBooks
www.oxfordowl.co.uk

Contents

Lost or Stolen?

Narinder Dhami

Chandra and her brother Ravi dreaded their cousin Taj coming to visit. During the summer holidays he was at their house almost every day because his parents worked long hours. He was there now, talking **incessantly** while they were trying to watch TV.

"See my new watch?" Taj waved his wrist under Ravi's nose. "It was really expensive!"

Chandra and Ravi exchanged **exasperated** glances. Taj hadn't stopped boasting since he'd arrived. He was *such* a show-off!

"Mum bought me these cool trainers yesterday, too." Taj waggled his feet. "I've got about eighty pairs of trainers now!"

"Who cares?" Chandra muttered.

Ravi sighed heavily. Taj's parents had loads of money and gave him whatever he wanted – the newest, the best and the most expensive of *everything*. Ravi had had just about enough of Taj's smugness.

"Well, I've got something to show *you*, Taj!" Ravi snapped. He went over to the table and picked up a gleaming silver handheld games console. "Check this out!"

Taj's mouth fell open. "But that's the KZY Version 4!" he said, astounded. "It's not available in the shops yet. How did *you* get it?"

"Our dad's friend works for the company in the USA," Ravi replied. "He sent me one."

"*I'm* getting one, too, as soon as they're on sale," Taj retorted sulkily. "Anyway, you shouldn't brag about it, Ravi!"

"What...?" Ravi spluttered, lost for words.

"Tea's ready," Mum called from the kitchen.

"Can you *believe* what Taj just said?" Ravi hissed to Chandra as they left the living room. "What a cheek!"

Chandra giggled. "At least you've got something he hasn't, just for once!" she replied.

After tea they played football in the garden.

"I'm getting new football boots with gold laces," Taj boasted. "Some of the Premiership footballers wear them!"

Chandra and Ravi were extremely relieved when Taj's dad arrived to collect him.

"Bye, Taj," said Mum. "See you tomorrow."

"Oh no, Mum!" Chandra groaned. "It's Raksha Bandhan tomorrow, remember?"

Chandra loved Raksha Bandhan, a festival celebrating brothers and sisters. Every year she tied a *rakhi*, a golden silk thread, around her brother's wrist and gave him sweets. Ravi would give Chandra a present, maybe some money or a pair of earrings.

Then their parents would take them out for the day. It wouldn't be a special treat, though, if big-mouth Taj was visiting, Chandra thought.

"Girls give *rakhis* to their boy cousins, too," Mum explained. "You can tie a *rakhi* on Taj."

Chandra pulled a face. "Do I have to?"

"I know Taj can be hard work," Mum said, "but be kind to him. He's not as fortunate as you two."

"What's Mum talking about?" Ravi whispered to Chandra. "Taj gets everything he wants!"

Later that day Chandra was reading in her bedroom when Ravi hurtled into her room without knocking.

"My KZY4's vanished!" Ravi exclaimed. "I've searched everywhere for it."

Chandra closed her book. "Have you asked Mum if she's seen it?"

"You're joking, right?" Ravi rolled his eyes. "Mum and Dad made me promise *faithfully* to look after it. I'm dead if I don't find it!"

"That's because you always lose stuff," Chandra pointed out.

"I *haven't* lost it," Ravi retorted. "I'm sure Taj took it!"

Chandra was shocked. "You don't have any proof, Ravi."

"Well, I left it in the living room and Taj was the last one out when Mum called us for tea. He *must* have taken it!"

"Taj *was* very jealous," Chandra agreed. "But why would he steal it? He'll get one when it goes on sale, anyway."

"Yeah, but Taj *always* has to have things straight away," Ravi replied. "Or maybe he was being mean. Whatever. I just want my KZY4 back!"

"I'll help you look for it," Chandra said. "Maybe we'll find it before Taj comes tomorrow…"

The following day was Raksha Bandhan. The sun shone as brightly as the gold *rakhi* Chandra tied on Ravi's wrist. Ravi gave her a necklace, then they shared delicious Indian jellied sweets that glistened like rubies, emeralds and amethysts. But a sense of **trepidation** hung over Chandra and Ravi during the celebrations. Ravi was still convinced that Taj had taken his games console. Chandra was worried about what would happen when Taj arrived.

Taj looked **despondent** when he turned up, so despondent that Chandra and even Ravi felt a bit sorry for him.

"What's up?" asked Ravi suspiciously. Maybe Taj was feeling ashamed because he'd stolen the KZY4, he thought.

"My parents were going to take me to the fair later today," Taj muttered unhappily, "but they can't get time off work."

Chandra and Ravi suddenly realised what Mum had meant. Taj *didn't* get everything he wanted.

"I *can't* ask Taj if he took my KZY4," Ravi murmured to Chandra. "Look at his face – he might burst into tears!"

"I've got an idea," Chandra said thoughtfully.

Mum had given Chandra an extra *rakhi* with gold and green threads. Quickly, she tied it onto Taj's wrist.

"I know it's Raksha Bandhan," Taj said, surprised, "but I'm not your brother."

"Girls can give *rakhis* to their boy cousins," Chandra explained, handing Taj some sweets. "Anyway, you're here so much, you're *almost* like a brother!"

"Thanks Chandra," Taj sighed. "I wish I had a sister."

Chandra knew that Ravi was still bursting to ask Taj about the console.

"Look Taj," he blurted out. "We…"

"We always have a day out for Raksha Bandhan," said Chandra, butting in before Ravi could finish. "We could *all* go to the fair."

"Really?" Taj gasped, his face lighting up.

"*If* you promise not to keep bragging all the time!" Chandra shot back with a grin.

"Sorry," Taj mumbled, embarrassed. "I know I go on a bit. I'll try not to!" Then he turned to Ravi eagerly. "Can we try out your KZY4? I'm dying to have a go!"

"Um…" Ravi was flabbergasted. Taj *hadn't* taken his KZY4. So where was it?

Just then Dad came into the living room, and Ravi's eyes almost popped out of his head. Dad was holding his KZY4!

"Sorry, I borrowed this yesterday to have a go, and I forgot to give it back!" Dad confessed a little sheepishly.

"Thanks, Dad!" Ravi said. Relieved, he beamed at Chandra. Ravi was so glad he hadn't accused Taj without any proof. Now they could have a great day out, and for once, Taj had stopped boasting. Brilliant!

GADGET Magic

The magazine with all the latest news from the gadget world

What's in store in this month's *Gadget Magic*?

p.4

Special Feature

What does *Gadget Magic* think is **The Greatest Gadget of Them All?** Why not post your own opinions on our online Message Board!

p.6

Grandad's Gizmos

We look at how gadgets used to be!

1956: The first computer with a hard disk. It weighed over a ton and could store just 4 megabytes – enough for one song!

p.10

Watch Out!

Want a watch that does more than tell the time? Check out *Gadget Magic's* selection of the latest top features!

▶ **Fitness freaks**: Monitor yourself running to school. Top speed? Heart rate? Distance? Compare today's results with yesterday's!

▶ **Built-in weather sensors**: Will you be splashing on the sun cream or pulling on the wellies?

▶ **Surf dudes**: Find tide times for the local beaches, wherever you are in the world.

Funky Future?

p.14

We take a look at some wacky ideas for gadgets of the future, still in the very early stages of development.

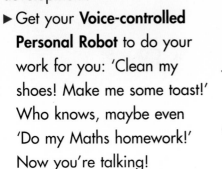

► Get your **Voice-controlled Personal Robot** to do your work for you: 'Clean my shoes! Make me some toast!' Who knows, maybe even 'Do my Maths homework!' Now you're talking!

► **Holo-World**: Do your school work without leaving the comfort of your favourite armchair – lessons will be accessed through a Wi-Fi Internet connection. No desks, no telling off, no school dinners. Amazing!

► The **Brain Box**: Ask it any question and it'll supply the answer. 'What's the capital of Australia? Where are my clean socks? Why is my sister such a pest?'

I-Spy!

p.28

Choose your favourite from our pick of the best-ever spy gadgets. We've got hollowed-out coins that can hide a tiny storage card, cameras concealed in buttons, glasses that let you see in the dark and James Bond's unforgettable jet pack!

Next month: SNEAK PREVIEW SPEC-tacular!

These glasses have an in-built computer, phone and microphone. Info flashes up in front of your eyes, and Voice Command gives you full control over the functions. Pretty eye-catching, huh?

▶ ▶ ▶ ▶ ▶ ▶ The Greatest Gadget of Them All? ◀ ◀ ◀ ◀ ◀ ◀

What does *Gadget Magic* consider to be The Greatest Gadget of Them All? Our winner is the mighty smart phone, and this familiar tale will show you why.

Disaster! The car is stuck in a huge traffic jam. There's little chance now of reaching the airport in time to catch their flight to Glasgow. Ellie snuggles up in the back seat as her dad grumbles and chunters. The wait's no problem for her – she's got her smart phone.

How should she pass the time? Well, how about listening to some of the 500 songs stored in her music folder, or reading one of the books she has in her online library? What about a crossword or sudoku puzzle?

Maybe she'll watch a video, or catch up on some of the TV shows she's missing, or have one more go at reaching level 13 of Super Dragon Quest.

Finger getting tired by now? Not to worry, with Voice Control she can just tell her phone what to do. Magic!

These are just a few of the functions that make the smart phone The Greatest Gadget of Them All.

Even if they are stuck in the traffic jam, Ellie can use the Internet on her phone to find new flight times and then her mum can book and pay online. How much will it cost for the whole family? The calculator app will sort that out. They'll be arriving at a different time now, so she'd better text her uncle to let him know when to pick them up. What about her cousin Sophie's party tonight? They'll be expecting her. No problem – she can use a social networking site to let her friends know she'll be late.

Then she has a brainwave. What about the satnav installed on her phone? Can it find another route to the airport? *"Turn right in 20 metres."* Yippee! Even Dad's impressed. Now he can stop moaning and start driving. Looks like they'll catch that plane after all. Time to relax and take a nap.

But what's that ringing sound disturbing Ellie's happy snooze? Oh yes, I nearly forgot. You can make phone calls on it too. *"Hi, Uncle Jack! You got my text then…?"*

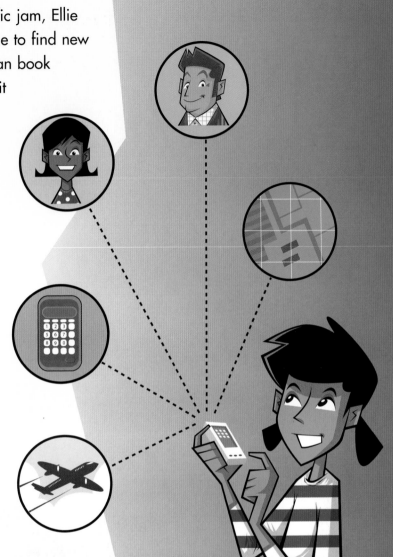

Why the smart phone is our worthy winner:
► it has multiple features
► it is entertaining
► you are connected to the Internet
► everything you need is in one handy gadget.

Can anything beat it? Add your opinion to our online Message Board.

The Balloons

Against these turbid* turquoise skies
    The light and luminous balloons
    Dip and drift like satin moons,
Drift like silken butterflies;

Reel with every windy gust,
    Rise and reel like dancing girls,
    Float like strange transparent pearls,
Fall and float like silver dust.

Oscar Wilde

* thick and misty

My Sari

Saris hang on the washing line:

a rainbow in our neighbourhood.

This little orange one is mine,

it has a mango leaf design.

I wear it as a Rani* would.

It wraps around me like sunshine,

it ripples silky down my spine,

and I stand tall and feel so good.

Debjani Chatterjee

* an Indian queen

At the End of a School Day

It is the end of a school day
        and down the long drive
come bag-swinging, shouting children.
        Deafened, the sky winces.
            The sun gapes in surprise.

Suddenly, the runners skid to a stop,
        stand still and stare
at a small hedgehog
        curled up on the tarmac
            like an old, frayed cricket ball.

A girl dumps her bag, tiptoes forward
        and gingerly, so gingerly
carries the creature
        to the safety of a shady hedge.
            Then steps back, watching.

Girl, children, sky and sun
　　hold their breath.
There is a silence,
　　a moment to remember
　　　　on this warm afternoon in June.

Wes Magee

Home | UFO sightings

Your Alien Experiences

Miss J.L. from Torbay:

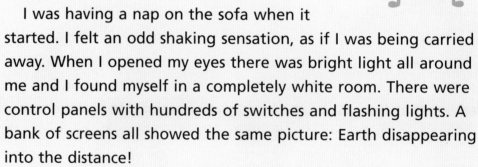

I used to laugh at some of the stories on this website, but not now. You see, two weeks ago I was taken aboard an alien spacecraft.

I was having a nap on the sofa when it started. I felt an odd shaking sensation, as if I was being carried away. When I opened my eyes there was bright light all around me and I found myself in a completely white room. There were control panels with hundreds of switches and flashing lights. A bank of screens all showed the same picture: Earth disappearing into the distance!

After a few seconds I noticed someone watching me from across the room. He (though it could have been a she) looked very much like a human, but slightly smaller. His head was much larger than ours though, and completely bald. He had bright green eyes and a tiny, pointed nose.

An artist's impression of the alien and its spacecraft

Photos	Scientific information

He didn't make any sound, but I felt like he was asking me questions. I told him all about myself – my childhood, my family, my job, England, the world. While I was talking he didn't move a muscle, but I could hear a faint whirring sound, as if everything I said was being recorded and analysed. When I'd finished he looked at me closely. Was he smiling? At once I felt myself sinking into a dreamless sleep.

When I woke up I was lying in the middle of a field. It was half past two, exactly the time I'd fallen asleep on the sofa. I don't know who or what it was that took me away, and I don't know where they took me. I don't suppose I'll ever find out. But I remember that final look, and I can't help thinking that somehow they liked me. Maybe that's why I'm still around to tell my story.

What do aliens look like?
View our artist's impressions based on your experiences.

Seen a UFO? Send us your photos

Do you have an alien story to tell?
Click here to contact us

23

The Daily Blab

SCHOOL PLAYGROUND USED FOR ALIEN KICKABOUT!

An alien football has been found on a Bristol school playground. UFO expert, Dr Marvin Spong, declared: "This is the latest and clearest proof that we are not alone!"

Dr Marvin Spong: *Expert on all things alien*

Sid Perry, caretaker of Clifton Primary School, made the dramatic discovery as dawn broke on Monday morning.

"I could hardly believe my eyes!" he gasped later. "Twenty years I've been working here, and I've seen most things, but this tops the lot!"

The abandoned football was made of smooth, brown rock. Were the visiting Martians disturbed during their fantasy football match? Head teacher Suzy Adams was so startled that she immediately called the police.

Suzy Adams: *Has no doubt that the mysterious rock is an alien football*

Whistling

As they questioned locals, a clear picture began to emerge. Although nobody actually saw the space invaders, several people were woken by odd whistling sounds in the night. Was this the alien craft making its landing, or did they even bring their own astro-referee?

One child at the school claimed that the streetlights started "flickering in a weird sort of way" at exactly nine o'clock on Sunday evening. In Dr Spong's expert opinion this was almost certainly due to the magnetic effects of the spacecraft as it made its final approach.

Red Lion: *The scene of a previous UFO sighting*

UFO

The area has seen many other alien-related incidents. In November 2007 a UFO was spotted outside the Red Lion Hotel, glowing bright blue before disappearing in a flash over the rooftops. Last June, two Year 4 children vanished for over an hour while on a school trip to a local theme park – a clear case of alien kidnap.

Jordan Fall and Ryan Ellis: *Missing at the theme park for over an hour*

Later, they could remember nothing about it, as if their memories had been wiped clean! Now all we can do is wait to see if the football-mad aliens return for their lost ball. When they do, you'll read about it first here in *The Daily Blab*!

The Bogey Men
and the
Trolls Next Door

Kaye Umansky

1 Hello! I'm Fred the Bogeyman.
   I live beside the bog
   With my bogey wife and kiddies
   And my faithful bogey dog.

2 Now, this is Mrs Bogey
   In her baggy bogey frock
   And her big, black, bogey bovver boots,
   Posing by a rock.

3 (When it comes to breaking rocks up,
   Mrs Bogey is the guv.
   Her name is really Beryl,
   But I always call her "luv".)

4 Here are our bogey children –
   Daphne, Bert and little Douggie...
   And here is Baby Bogey
   In his bogey baby buggy.

5 And this is Snot, our bogey dog.
   (We've taught him how to beg.)
   He eats a lot of bogey bones
   And sometimes bites your leg.

6 We're a happy little family.
  We lead a quiet life,
  Just minding our own business
  And avoiding stress and strife.

7 Yes, I'd say we were contented.
  Or at least we were before
  That very **fateful** evening
  When the Trolls moved in next door!

8 We were sitting down to supper
  With our bowls of bogey stew
  (Which is gooey, rather gluey,
  And quite difficult to chew) –

9 When a knock came on our cavern door.
  I said "Who can that be?"
  And a voice like grating gravel
  Very boomily said "Me!"

10 I opened up the door a crack.
   The Trolls stood just outside.
   They were rocky. They were cocky.
   They were weighty. They were *wide*.

11 "Hello! We're your new neighbours,"
   Boomed the biggest one. "I'm Dave.
   We've come to introduce ourselves.
   We're in the next-door cave."

12 "This here's my good wife Dolly.
   This is Colin, Mol and Polly...
   "And here's our trollish baby
   In her teeny trollish trolley.

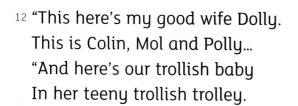

13 And last, not least, meet Tiddles,
   Our charming trollish cat.
   I wonder, could we step inside
   And have a friendly chat?"

14 I simply stood and stared at them.
   I did not say "How do?"
   I did not say, "Do come on in
   And have some bogey stew."

15 I *glared*. I bared my *teeth* at them.
   I don't like Trolls one bit,
   And wanted to be really sure
   They were aware of it.

16 "I'm sorry," I said coldly,
   With my baddest bogey sneer,
   "Us Bogeys do not like you Trolls.
   We don't want Trolls round here.

17 "You don't control your children.
   You like to scream and fight,
   You play loud trollish music
   Very late into the night.

18 "Well, that is what I've heard, and I'm
   Quite sure that it is true."
   And I firmly shut the door on them
   And went back to my stew.

19 Well, that was the beginning.
   From then on, things went downhill.
   Between us and our neighbours
   Fell an atmosphere of chill.

20 And, as the weeks and months went by,
Things slowly got more tense.
The children pulled rude faces
Across the garden fence.

21 The cat and dog were enemies.
They did a lot of spitting.
The wives were coldly critical
About each other's knitting.

22 And me and Dave would shake our fists
If ever we should meet
(When we'd been to shop for groceries)
Accidentally, in the street.

23 The Trolls held noisy parties
And us Bogeys would complain.
But they'd laugh right in our faces
Then they'd do it all again.

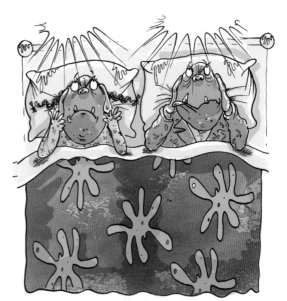

24 They invited their relations
For a sing-song every week,
And bellowed anti-Bogey songs,
Which was an awful cheek.

25 Their children broke our windows
With their heavy trollish balls
And at night, they took their hammers out
And hammered on our walls!

26 Us Bogeys got our own back.
We would sneak on out at dawn
And dump our bogey rubbish
On their tidy trollish lawn.

27 We muddied up their washing
And we trampled on their flowers,
Then acted most **indignant**
When they came and trampled ours!

28 We smothered all their doorknobs
With bogey superglue.
We had to scare them off, you see,
For that's what Bogeys *do*.

29 We were sitting down to breakfast
Eating bogey toast and jam,
And our darling Baby Bogey
Was out dozing in his pram.

30 (We often leave him out there
In the garden, where it's sunny,
Blowing bogey baby bubbles
And burbling to his bunny.)

31 "I'll go and check the baby,"
Mrs Bogey firmly said.
"I think he might be sleeping.
I'll just pop him in his bed."

32 And she strode into the garden.
Then we heard a frightened shout...
"Help, everyone! Come quickly!
Baby Bogey has got out!"

33 It was true. His pram was empty.
What a very nasty shock.
And over by the garden gate
(Which we forgot to lock)...

34 We saw little baby footprints
Which we stared at, all agog,
For they led in the direction
Of the dreaded Bogey Bog!

35 The Bogey Bog! The Bogey Bog!
A place of mud and murk,
All bristling with Danger signs
And snakes, and Things that Lurk.

36 A stagnant stretch of quagmire,
Very **desolate** and grim.
No place for bogey babies
Who have not been taught to swim!

37 Just then, we heard a startled scream –
And, to our great surprise
The Trolls next door came running out
With wildly rolling eyes.

38 "Have you Bogies seen our Baby?"
Came the chilling trollish cry,
"Our baby has gone missing!"
"Ours has too!" was our reply.

39 "They must have gone together,"
Dave the Troll then grimly said.
"We had better go and find them.
Will you come and help me, Fred?"

40 What a frenzy! What a panic!
We were well and truly worried,
And down towards the dreaded Bog
Us Trolls and Bogies hurried,

41 And we quite forgot to argue,
And we didn't fight or brawl.
This was a time of crisis –
All for one and one for all!

DANGER

BEWARE
OF
SNAKES

42 At last, we reached the Bogey Bog,
Our dreaded **destination** –
We were worn out to a frazzle
And quite drenched with perspiration...

43 And there we spied our babies
With mud up to their eyes,
Paddling in a puddle,
Busy making muddy pies!

44 We simply stood and looked at them,
So happy in their game.
Then we looked at one another –
And we hung our heads in shame.

45 The time had come to call a truce
And try to make amends.
From that moment onwards
We became the best of friends.

46 Now the children play together
And they have a lot of fun.
The wives sit drinking coffee
In the garden, in the sun.

47 Dave lends me his mower.
I lend Dave my axe,
And when we meet out shopping,
Well, we clap each other's backs!

48 The Trolls still hold their parties
And they like to sing at night –
But us Bogeys get invited too,
So that is quite all right.

49 The fence between our gardens
Fell down the other day –
But we haven't put it up again.
We like the fence that way.

50 Everything is peaceful now.
No more need for war.

Life is so much better
Since the Trolls moved in next door.

The Stellar Stage School

Is stage school for you? Follow our flow chart to find out.

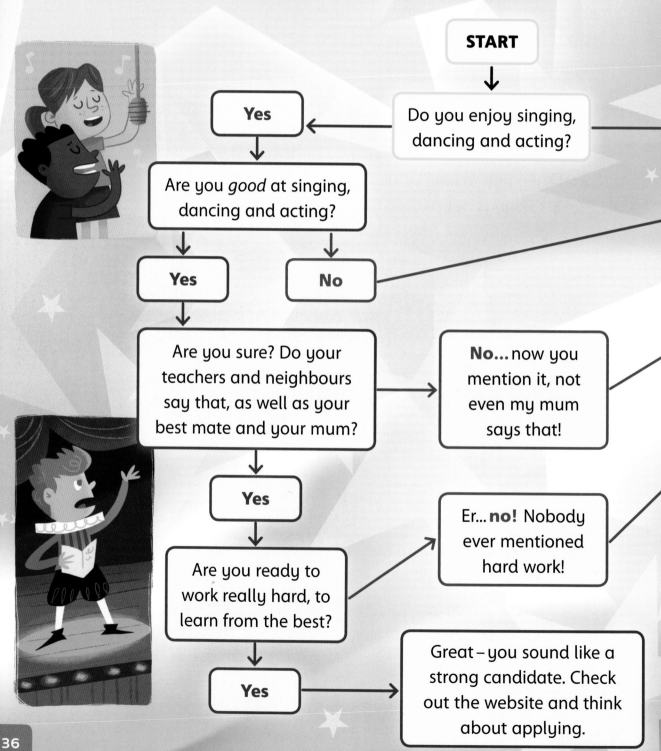

START

Do you enjoy singing, dancing and acting?

Yes

Are you *good* at singing, dancing and acting?

Yes

No

Are you sure? Do your teachers and neighbours say that, as well as your best mate and your mum?

No... now you mention it, not even my mum says that!

Yes

Er... **no!** Nobody ever mentioned hard work!

Are you ready to work really hard, to learn from the best?

Yes

Great – you sound like a strong candidate. Check out the website and think about applying.

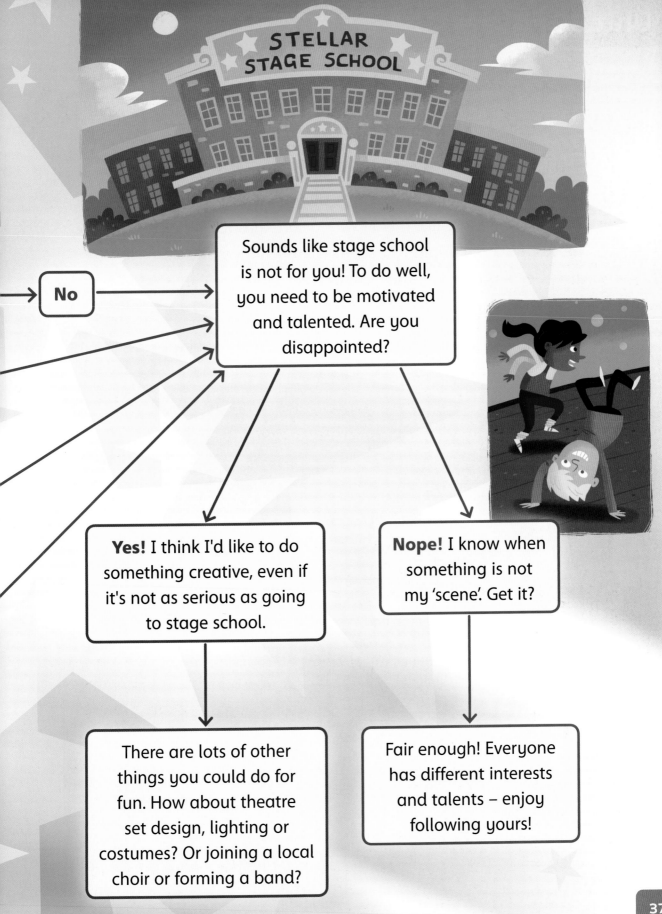

STELLAR STAGE SCHOOL

No

Sounds like stage school is not for you! To do well, you need to be motivated and talented. Are you disappointed?

Yes! I think I'd like to do something creative, even if it's not as serious as going to stage school.

Nope! I know when something is not my 'scene'. Get it?

There are lots of other things you could do for fun. How about theatre set design, lighting or costumes? Or joining a local choir or forming a band?

Fair enough! Everyone has different interests and talents – enjoy following yours!

Miss Lark's Lesson:
How the Voice Works

Ever wondered why some people sing beautifully, while others sound more like a wolf with a sore throat? To help the stage school pupils to become better singers, Miss Lark is explaining how the human voice works.

1. Something called a **diaphragm** squeezes air out of your lungs and up your **trachea** (windpipe).

2. On its way through your throat, this air passes through two little flaps of skin — you might know these as your **vocal cords**. They vibrate to make a sound. Simple!

3. The longer the vocal cords, the deeper the voice. Throat muscles can make the vocal cords s-t-r-e-t-c-h to make different sounds.

4. To change the sounds, try moving your jaw, cheeks, tongue and lips, like this. This also gives everyone else a laugh when they see the faces you're pulling!

How the Voice Works

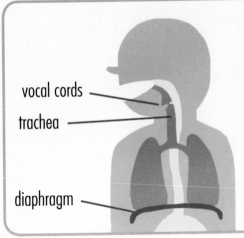

Miss Lark

Human voice glossary:

diaphragm (say it like this: **dye**-uh-fram)
– *a layer of muscle between your lungs and your stomach*

trachea (say it like this: **tra**-key-uh)
– *the tube connecting your throat to your lungs*

vocal cords – *two flaps of skin in your throat that vibrate to make sounds*

vocal cords

trachea

diaphragm

Are people born with a talent for singing?

Pop star brothers and sisters such as The Jonas Brothers or Kylie and Dannii Minogue might make you think there is a magic musical gene. On the other hand, it's quite common for one child to have a beautiful voice, while their brother or sister will have you covering your ears!

Scientists are researching whether musical talent runs in families, but they don't know what the answer is yet. One thing is for sure – all the best musicians work hard to develop their talent.

Top Tips on improving your singing voice

Good singers:

★ learn breathing techniques that allow them to produce just the right airflow at just the right time

★ train the muscles of their mouth and face so that they can get exactly the right mouth shape to make the sound they want

★ practise, practise, practise!

Stage school homework:
Make a sound and try moving your jaw, cheeks, tongue and lips around.
Listen to the sound change.
Watch yourself in the mirror.

The Fly and the Fool
Inspired by a Vietnamese folk tale

Lou Kuenzler

Characters

The Judge

a fair and honest man

Mr Lo

*a rich but **deceitful** merchant*

Lan

a clever village boy who loves telling riddles

Kym

his high-spirited sister

*In an outdoor meeting place. The Judge leans on a large, **imposing** desk. To his left sits Lan and to his right Mr Lo, who looks very cross. The actors should treat the audience as if they are local people watching the trial. Kym sits amongst this crowd.*

Judge (*To audience*) Quiet please. Settle down. (*Turning to Lan*) What is your complaint, lad? Tell the court why you are here.

Lan (*Stands, nervously*) Please, Your Honour, I want to complain about this man. (*He points at Mr Lo.*)

Mr Lo (*Jumping to his feet*) Surely the court will not waste time listening to a little grasshopper like this! I am a respectable businessman.

Judge The court has a duty to protect everyone, Mr Lo, the young and old, the rich and poor...

Mr Lo   (*Edging towards the Judge's table, whispering*) I am *very* rich, you know. If Your Honour needs a loan... just say the word.

Kym   (*Leaping up from the audience*) He's trying to give you money, Mr Judge, so you won't listen to what we have to say!

Judge   (*Firmly*) Order in the court! Sit down, young lady!

Kym   Sorry. (*She sits.*)

Judge   (*Turning back to Mr Lo*) But I do recognise a bribe when I hear one... I do NOT want to hear any more of them in this court. Understood?

Mr Lo nods, guiltily.

Judge   I believe we are here because of a loan.

Lan   Yes, Your Honour. Our family is not rich.

Kym   We're very poor! Sometimes we don't even have money for food.

Lan   My parents borrowed some money from Mr Lo. Just enough to buy something to eat until our rice harvest came in. But, when the harvest was over and we went to pay him back, he said the money was not enough.

Kym   (*On her feet again*) He said we owed him twice as much now!

Judge   Young lady! Compose yourself.

Kym   (*Sits, grumbling*) I was only trying to say...

Mr Lo   See the kind of ruffians we are dealing with! They've no respect for authority, whereas I am a fine, upstanding member of the community...

Lan   After a year, Mr Lo said we owed him *ten times* the amount my parents had borrowed!

Mr Lo   (*Shrugs*) I'm a businessman! I need to make a profit!

Judge   (*To Lan*) You say Mr Lo called at your cottage yesterday. Tell me what happened.

Lan   Kym and I were sweeping the path. (*He raises his eyebrows.*) She was pestering me as usual!

Kym comes out of the audience. The two children re-enact the scene, miming sweeping.

Kym   Tell me a riddle, Lan...*please!* You know I can *never* guess the answers.

Lan   All right! (*He thinks for a moment and then begins to walk slowly up and down the dusty path.*) Here's one: the more I take, the more I leave behind. What are they?

Judge   (*Clapping his hands, excited*) I'm **immensely** fond of riddles!

Kym   (*Shaking her head*) The more you take, the more you leave behind? I don't know...

Lan   It's footsteps. (*He paces again.*) The more I *take,* the more I *leave* behind. See! (*He points at his prints on the dusty path.*)

Judge   Very clever! Footsteps! I like that.

Mr Lo   It's just a childish riddle!

Kym   That's not what you said yesterday! You were desperate to solve riddles then.

Judge   (*Shaking his head at Kym*) I suppose it is useless to ask you to sit down, young lady?

Kym   I'll show you what happened! I'll pretend to be Mr Lo. Watch!

Kym rubs her belly and walks with her legs apart like a frog. The Judge tries not to laugh.

Mr Lo   This is outrageous!

◆ ◆ ◆

A re-enactment. Kym stays in character as Mr Lo.

Kym (as Mr Lo) (*Talking in a deep voice as she waddles around*) Are your **worthless** parents at home? I've come to collect the money they owe me.

Lan (*Winking*) I'll answer that with a riddle... My father has gone to cut living trees and plant dead ones!

Kym (as Mr Lo) (*Scratching her head*) What nonsense! Where's your mother?

Lan She's at the market, selling the wind and buying bright moonlight!

Kym (as Mr Lo) You're talking gibberish, boy!

Lan Not gibberish! Riddles...

Kym (as Mr Lo) Answer me plainly! Where have your parents gone?

Lan If I tell you the answer to my riddles, will you let my family off the money we owe?

Kym (as Mr Lo) Certainly not! I'm much cleverer than you. I'll solve your silly riddle for myself.

Kym mumbles in character, scratching her head even more.

...cut living trees and plant dead ones. Buy bright moonlight?... No! It's useless! Tell me the answer, boy!

Lan And you'll stop asking my parents for the money?

Kym (as Mr Lo) I promise! Just tell me the answer.

Lan We'll need a witness to our deal.

Kym (as Mr Lo) (*Smugly*) Fine! How about that fly that has just landed on the gate post?

They shake hands.

Lan All right. I'll tell you the answer to my riddles... My father's gone to cut living trees and plant dead ones! That means he went to cut down bamboo and make a fence with it!

Judge   I see. The bamboo is alive, but the fence will be dead! Brilliant!

Lan   My mother's at the market, selling the wind and buying bright moonlight. She's selling paper fans – which will give a cool breeze – so she can buy oil to light our lamps and make them shine brightly at night!

Kym (as Mr Lo)   Very clever! (*Under her breath, as if Mr Lo is whispering*) But you're a fool, boy, if you think a fly can be a witness.

The re-enactment ends. Lan and Kym approach the Judge again.

Kym   I promise, that's how it happened.

Lan   Later, when my parents went to thank Mr Lo for letting them off the money they owed, he pretended he had never spoken to me.

Mr Lo   (*Leaping up*) There never was a deal. It's nonsense! Your family still owes me money!

Lan   (*Smiles, cleverly*) But the fly was our witness. It landed right on the end of your nose, remember?

Kym   Buzzzzzzz! (*She taps Mr Lo's nose.*) Right there!

Mr Lo   That's a lie! The fly was not on my nose! It was on the gate like you said!

Kym and Lan   (*Together*) Ha!

Judge   (*Sternly*) Since you remember where the fly was, Mr Lo, you must also remember making your promise! These children are telling the truth. You made a deal and this family are now free of their debt!

Mr Lo   Oh no! (*He buries his head in his hands and groans.*) I tripped up on my own stupid lies. It is not the boy who is the fool...it is me!

Judge   (*To audience*) All those who agree, raise your hands!

Kym and Lan   Hurray!

JUNIOR DETECTIVE!

Do you have what it takes to be a detective one day?
How would you solve this practice case?

The case

Jet-setting celebrities Dexter and Dara Corbett arrived back from their trip to New York to find a scene of total devastation. Thieves had broken in through the back door of their mansion, disabled the alarm and CCTV systems and blown open the safe. Thousands of pounds worth of diamonds had been stolen.

Could you find the criminals? Think about what steps you would take to solve the crime, then check with the expert tips below.

Tip 1: Search for clues at the scene of the crime. A squad of specialist officers will help you look for evidence. This could appear in many forms: blood stains, hairs, fibres from clothes, fingerprints or even footprints. Sometimes these clues are tiny, almost invisible to the human eye, so get your magnifying glass out!

Crime Scene Investigators (CSIs) wear plastic suits to make sure that they don't leave their own DNA traces at the scene. Any fingerprints they find can be checked against the computerised criminal database. However, the thieves may have worn gloves.

The CSI team will also look for samples of **DNA** that the thieves may have left behind. Every person's body has a unique DNA code, which can be found in their blood, hair, skin, sweat and saliva. The tiniest fibre from someone's clothing can contain traces of their DNA.

A DNA sample can't prove that a person committed the crime, but it will prove without doubt that they were at the scene.

Watch out!

Identical twins have the same DNA. Also a clever criminal might try to plant DNA from another person at the crime scene.

Tip 2: Interview anyone who might be able to help, such as the victims, their family, the cleaner or gardener, neighbours or passers-by. You might even appeal for help on a TV crime programme. Try filming a reconstruction of the crime to jog people's memories. Did anyone see or hear anything unusual?

Watch out!

Some people may not have good memories or might try to deliberately 'frame' another person to pass the blame on to them.

Tip 3: Sift through all the evidence to try to find suspects.

Who might have had a reason (we call this a **motive**) to commit the crime? It could have been someone who needed money or someone who had a grudge against the victims.

Who had the necessary tools to break into the house? Did they buy them from a local shop? The shopkeepers might remember, so you should talk to them too. Does the crime follow the same pattern as any previous robberies?

Who was in the area when the crime was committed? If a suspect can prove they were somewhere else entirely (we call this an **alibi**), you can cross them off your list.

Watch out!

Don't be fooled by a false alibi. It's possible the suspect asked someone to lie for them, so check out their story!

Just, er, fixing the wheel on my bike.

LOOT

Watch out!

Your suspect may be using another person's identity – you'll need to be smart to keep one step ahead of them.

Tip 4: Think you know who committed the crime? Now all you've got to do is find them!

You may be able to obtain photos of them that you can show on TV. If not, police artists and computer experts can put together images which are nearly as good as a photo. Try to trace the cars they might be driving, and make sure to check airport flight lists – you don't want them to leave the country and escape.

Tip 5: Once you've found them, go and arrest them. After that you can interview them down at the police station. Watch out for tell-tale signs in their body language – fidgeting, mumbling and avoiding eye contact can all be signs that someone is lying. If your suspect frequently says 'to be honest' or 'to tell you the truth', research has suggested that they probably aren't!

Lie detectors

In some countries, police are allowed to put suspects through a lie detector test. When someone is lying, the stress causes tiny changes in their breathing and heart rate. They can be

wired up to a machine called a polygraph, which monitors these changes as they answer questions. If they're fibbing, they might be found out!

Watch out!

Some people might feel very nervous being interviewed and so look suspicious, even if they've not done anything wrong. Remember that the law states a suspect is innocent until proven guilty!

If you're lucky then your suspects might confess to the crime. If not, a judge and jury in court can decide whether you're right or wrong.

How did you do? Have you got what it takes to be a detective in the future?

Runaways!

Jim Eldridge

"Walk! Don't run!" Hannah hissed in a whisper to her brother. "Act like everything's normal."

The last thing they needed was someone shouting at them for running and bumping into people, thought 10-year-old Hannah, and for them to be caught and taken back. She and her brother, John, had managed to **steal out** of the workhouse just before the gates were secured for the night.

Hannah had been watching for their chance to escape ever since she'd overheard the Master of the Workhouse, Mr Patch, talking to the chimney sweep.

"I've got the perfect boy for you, Mr Parker," Patch had said. "His name's John Williams. He's eight years old, and thin as a rake. He'd go up chimneys as easy as a brush."

"He ain't a moaner, is he?" asked the sweep. "The last boy I had said the bricks were too hot, or the chimneys were too narrow, or he couldn't breathe because of the soot."

"No, no, Mr Parker," Patch assured the sweep. "Williams will be no trouble."

"What about the parents?" asked Parker.

"No parents to worry about," said Patch. "He's an orphan. He and his sister came to us when he was a baby and she were only two. We're the only family they've got."

Hannah nearly burst out in **fury** at the word 'family'. That was the last word she'd use to describe the workhouse. The food they were given barely kept them alive: gruel and dry bread. Hannah was sure that the dreadful conditions were why John was ill. His lungs were weak. If he was sent up chimneys every day, it could kill him.

That night they tried to sleep in the doorway of an old shop, but it didn't give them much shelter. A harsh wind blew and it began to rain. John coughed, his body shaking distressingly. Hannah took her coat off and wrapped it around him. She shivered, too cold to sleep.

As the sun came up the next morning, Hannah shook John awake, and they began to plod along the cobbled street. Her main concern was that Patch would send people out looking for them. After all, every child at the workhouse was worth money to him.

"I'm hungry," said John **despondently**.

They hadn't eaten since they'd left the workhouse.

"Don't worry," Hannah assured him. "I'll find us something."

But she knew that wouldn't be easy. Food cost money, and they didn't have any. She could try begging, but that might get the attention of the police, and then they'd be back inside the dreaded workhouse.

They **trudged** on until they came to Regent Street. The street was wide, with expensive shops and grand buildings on either side.

Hannah watched as an elegantly dressed man prepared to cross the road. As he stopped at the kerb, a young girl appeared beside him with a broom and began to clear a path through the horse droppings that covered the roadway. With so much horse-drawn traffic in London, rich people needed these crossing-sweepers if they were to get from one side of a road to the other without getting muck on their shoes and the bottom of their clothes.

Hannah watched as the girl accepted a coin the man gave her. She hurried over to the girl.

"Can I borrow your broom?" Hannah asked urgently.

The girl looked at her suspiciously. "Why?" she demanded.

"I need to earn some money to buy food for my brother." She pointed at John, who was coughing again. "I'll pay you for it, as soon as I get some money from someone. I only need to do one sweep."

The girl shook her head.

"If you want to get money without a broom, try being a mudlark," she said.

Hannah frowned, puzzled. "What's a mudlark?" she asked.

"The people who go down to the river when the tide's out and dig through the mud," said the girl. "They find stuff that people have dropped in the river, coins and old bits of iron, and then they flog it."

Night fell. Hannah and John were exhausted. They'd spent the daylight hours when the tide was out up to their knees in the thick oozing mud at the edges of the River Thames, searching for things to sell for scrap.

Hannah's pockets were heavy with objects they'd found: small bits of rusty iron, a piece of a broken horseshoe, but no coins. They still hadn't eaten.

That night Hannah and John found **refuge** in another shop doorway.

"I'm so starved!" croaked John.

"Tomorrow, we'll eat," she promised him. "We'll sell this stuff and get some money."

She cuddled him, doing her best to keep him warm against the night chill. She had to find somewhere safe, or John would die!

"So," said a deep voice. "What have we here?"

Hannah felt a bolt of fear go through her as she looked up at the well-dressed man and woman looking down at them. Patch's people had found them!

"Please, sir, I ain't done nothing wrong! Don't send us back!" she begged, beginning to cry. "We was hungry and my brother's ill, sir," she said through her tears. "He's gonna die if he don't get no food and shelter."

The man turned to the woman, a questioning look on his face. The woman nodded. Then they both looked at Hannah.

"My name is Dr Thomas Barnardo," said the man. "We can give you shelter and food."

Hannah looked up at them, instantly suspicious. She had heard about people who preyed on young street children.

"Here," said the woman, and Hannah saw she was holding out a paper bag. Hannah took it. Inside was some bread and cheese. Then the man, Dr Barnardo, held out a coin.

"This will buy you food tomorrow. If you come to our shelter in Stepney Causeway, you'll find a home with other children like yourselves, and you will be safe and cared for." He smiled at her. "I know you are **wary** of strangers, and rightly so; which is why we hope to see you tomorrow, in the light of day."

With that, Barnardo tipped his hat to Hannah, as if she was a proper lady, not a barefoot runaway.

"Tomorrow," he said. Then he and the woman walked on.

Hannah looked after them, **awed**. Then she smiled and gave John the bread and cheese, and cuddled him close.

"Eat up, John," she said. "I think we're gonna be all right!"

London 🦁👑🦁 Herald

The Victorian Voice of News and Progress

BUILDING WORK COMPLETED ON BARNARDO'S HOME FOR THE CITY'S STREET CHILDREN

One of London's most shameful sights may soon become a thing of the past, thanks to the will and determination of one man – Dr Thomas Barnardo.

Dr Barnardo has been working for some time towards his dream of ending the horror and misery of countless children by housing the homeless youngsters of London in safety and warmth. However, readers of this paper will know that the project to build a Dr Barnardo's Home was put on hold due to lack of funds. We are pleased to announce that Dr Barnardo's dream took a step closer to reality this week. Thanks to several generous offers of financial support, he is on the way to achieving this feat. Building work has now been completed and the first Dr Barnardo Home will open its doors in the autumn.

The problems facing young children in our capital have been reported many times by this newspaper. Our readers are always left seething when they find out how many children grow up in extremely unhealthy conditions, living in dirty, overcrowded rooms with no sanitation. They are often forced into highly unsuitable work to help to support their families.

Those without families may have to endure the dreadful conditions of the workhouse. Worst of all, the rest can be found outside any night of the week on rooftops, in doorways, under bridges – anywhere they might be able to find a place to sleep. Without the means to buy food, they are forced to beg or steal to continue their awful existence.

Dr Barnardo's aim is to find these stray, hopeless orphans and take them in.

Dr Barnardo's dream is that no destitute child will ever be turned away.

They will then be looked after and given an education until work can be found that matches their abilities, so that they can grow up and become productive members of society.

If the first home is successful, the doctor plans to expand his charitable operation and set up many more Dr Barnardo's Homes. For the sake of our great city of London, let us hope that he succeeds.

Social Diary

The well-known author **Charles Dickens** will read extracts from his popular novels, including the heart-warming tale of *Oliver Twist*, at the Savoy Hotel from 7.30 p.m. on Monday.

A **football match** between teams representing England and Scotland will be held on Saturday at the Kennington Oval ground. The organisers suggest that the occasion may not be suitable for ladies.

Mr Carlo Borlini will be offering tuition in the latest **ballroom dancing** techniques at the Langtree Tea Rooms on Wednesday afternoon. Accompaniment will be provided by the Hammersmith Dance Orchestra.

THIS SUMMER IN HISTORY

1851 Visitors flocked into the Crystal Palace to witness some of the marvels of the modern world in the Great Exhibition. Craftsmen and performers left audiences spellbound with their unique displays.

1866 Isambard Kingdom Brunel's steamship the *Great Eastern* completed the laying of an underground cable between England and the United States. The cable, lying on the bed of the Atlantic Ocean, was hailed a triumph. It allows messages to be sent between our two great nations in Morse code.

The MARVEL

The latest and most excellent bicycle for gentlemen, now fitted with rubber tyres and pedals. Experience the thrill of the utmost in speed and comfort!

To place an order, please send £10 to Crabtree's Cycles, High Street, Muswell Hill, London.

Boyle's Chocolate Peppermint bar

Your boys and girls are sure to turn their noses up at any other chocolate bar after they've tasted Boyle's Chocolate Peppermint bar.

Silky smooth peppermint cream, wrapped in a thick layer of delicious dark chocolate.

Toghill's Clockwork Train

Make your son's birthday dream come true with a finely crafted Clockwork Train from Toghill's. Just wind it up and watch it go!

Visit TOGHILL'S, makers of quality clockwork toys since 1826.

Sugarcane Juice

Pratima Mitchell

Hamid thought the bus station was the best place in the world. For him, revving engines sounded sweeter than music, and diesel fumes smelled better than flowers. His heart thrilled to the hustle and bustle of street sellers, the comings and goings of passengers. He saw people from every corner of Pakistan: tribesmen from the north, children of all ages, wedding parties…and the buses! Gorgeously painted in rainbow colours – **gaudy**, tasselled and tinselled. Once they left the station the buses picked up speed, thundering towards Islamabad, Karachi, Faisalabad and other towns. Faces crowded at the windows, hands waved goodbye and extra passengers perched perilously on luggage racks.

After school Hamid always raced to the bus station to help his father and his father's friends. Abba, his dad, owned a cart fitted with a machine for pressing sugarcane juice. The cart was a work of art, decorated with red flowers, green hills and blue clouds. On the front were two lights, painted like eyes that always looked like they held a secret. On the top there was a hand juicer, a row of glasses and a pile of greeny-yellow sugarcane.

The man who sold peanuts would call, "Hey Hamid, give us a hand. Hurry up! That bus for Wagah leaves in five minutes!" So Hamid would grab the tray of snacks and canter like a little pony to pass it under the windows of the departing bus. Paper cones of nuts and money were exchanged. Another of his father's pals would yell, "I need more milk for my tea stall! Here's ten rupees – quick, go and get me some."

Every day was like this. Hamid was everyone's favourite because he could be trusted with money and relied on to be polite and make sales.

While the buses waited for passengers to board and settle down, salesmen also clambered up with their goods. There were men selling medicines that claimed to cure anything, *anything at all.*

"Pimples, headaches, blindness, earache, lovesickness, chickenpox...whatever your illness, my wonder oil will put you right!"

Others sold bracelets and rings, bananas, mangoes and fizzy drinks. Hamid's favourite was Bulbul the conjurer, who could do the most amazing tricks.

One afternoon, when Hamid arrived at the bus station, everyone seemed to be in a bad temper. Perhaps it was the blazing sun, which glared down like a sheet of brass.

"You took your time," grumbled Abba. "Help me by taking around this tray of sugarcane juice." He handed Hamid a wire tray with six glasses of cloudy green juice. "Remember, two rupees a glass."

Hamid wound his way through the crowds of passengers. He caught a glimpse of Bulbul hopping on to the bus that said 'Timarpur'. Carefully balancing his wire tray of glasses with his left hand, Hamid climbed up the steps and greeted the driver and conductor with "Salam Alaikum".

In the central aisle Bulbul was producing one coloured handkerchief after another. All around him passengers continued to arrange their bags, their children and their animals.

Hamid forgot about selling his juice. He stood open-mouthed as Bulbul swallowed egg after egg. Then, tiny yellow chicks seemed to multiply from a hat.

Hamid applauded, forgetting the tray and slopping sugarcane juice over a lady.

"*Hut, badmash,* scoundrel!" she shouted, dabbing the damp patch with a scarf.

"Sorry, Bibiji."

"I'll 'Bibiji' you!" she cried.

In the confusion, Hamid didn't realise that Bulbul had already hopped off the bus. A baby chick was left cheeping on a rack and the bus was on its way to Timarpur!

"Stop, Uncle, stop!" shouted Hamid, but the bus was ancient and it groaned and creaked like an old person in pain, so the driver couldn't hear him. The bus **lurched** and swayed under its load of passengers, goats, chickens and baskets of vegetables and fruit. Hamid looked around helplessly. The interior was **festooned** with tinsel, shiny bunting and mirrors. The ceiling was painted like the night sky, with stars and a full moon, and there were vases of plastic flowers stuck to the sides. The flowers nodded busily. He managed to grab the chick and pocketed it for safety.

Nobody paid attention to the young boy with a tray of sugarcane juice. One bold man stretched out and helped himself to a drink. Quick as a flash Hamid held out his hand, "Two rupees, if you please."

Reluctantly the man slapped the coins in his waiting palm. Suddenly the bus jolted as it went over a bump. Hamid stumbled, dropping the tray. The glasses fell on the floor with a crash, splashing juice.

"Who is this boy?" grumbled one old man. "Driver, get this fellow off the bus. He's ruined my jacket!"

The driver glanced over his shoulder. "You still here? Get off at the next stop and go home."

Hamid was well and truly **rattled**; not just by his unwanted adventure, but also by the movement of the bus. All he wanted was to go back to Abba.

At the first stop, the driver let him off. "Have you enough money?"

Hamid checked his pockets. "Six rupees."

"That won't get you far. Here, take this. Twenty rupees – pay me back when I return tomorrow."

Hamid got off, carrying the tray – now full of empty, juice-smeared glasses. He was on a main road about ten miles from home. He'd never been so far from his familiar surroundings on his own. He was hot, sticky and hungry. He'd just have to wait until a bus appeared, going the other way. He stroked the chick gently and wished Bulbul was with him.

All kinds of traffic whizzed past throwing up clouds of dust – carts, camels, buffaloes, old cars, shiny new ones, bikes and motorbikes. Carefully crossing the road, Hamid found the bus stop and settled down in the shade.

The air cooled a little towards evening when a bus bound for his town slowed down to let him on. Hamid climbed up the steps and the driver recognised him.

"Hamid! Whatever are you doing here? Here, come and sit next to me. No, no, I don't want any money. Tell me what happened." The driver offered him some peanuts to munch.

Hamid told him the whole story.

The bus driver laughed merrily. "Isn't it lucky that we all know you and your father? Never mind, we'll soon be at the bus station. Now tell me – what will you be when you grow up?"

In a flash, out popped Hamid's answer: "A bus driver of course!"

Critic's Review:

VIPER!

VIPER! has the makings of a sure-fire blockbuster. All the ingredients are there: wicked villains, cunning plans, an unlikely young hero battling against the odds to save himself, his friends, and his country…and all the while the clock is ticking. A stunning performance by Andy Francis in the lead role marks him out as a definite star of the future.

VIPER! is highly recommended for cinema-goers looking for thrills, gripping action and heart-in-mouth suspense. But beware: if you're easily scared you'd better stay at home, because this film will have you on the edge of your seat, from the breathtaking opening action right up until the final dramatic twist.

VIPER! – don't miss it, or you'll regret it!

Gracie Smith, film critic,
The Manchester News

VIPER!   A Film Trailer

FADE IN:

EXTERIOR. DAY. AN ENGLISH VILLAGE IN SUMMER.
Shots of cottages, an old church, trees.

> NARRATOR (VOICE-OVER)
> Eastville…a sleepy village in the peaceful
> English countryside. But all is not what
> it seems. This village holds a secret - a
> terrifying secret…

Shot of ROAD CLOSED sign.

EXTERIOR. NIGHT.
Sudden flash to close-up on a snake.

INTERIOR. NIGHT.
Shots of members of VIPER.

> NARRATOR (VOICE-OVER)
> VIPER…a group of international criminals
> with one aim…to take over Britain.

EXTERIOR. NIGHT.
Zoom in on the eye of the snake.
Cut to shot of scientific code.

> NARRATOR (VOICE-OVER)
> Using the venom of a deadly snake, they've
> developed a nerve gas which can control minds…

INTERIOR. DAY. A LABORATORY.
Shot of scientists working with test tubes.

> NARRATOR (VOICE-OVER)
> …bringing people under their wicked spell,
> putting them completely in their power.
> Eastville was a test. Now they're ready for
> a bigger target.

EXTERIOR. DAY. LONDON.
Shots of Trafalgar Square, London buses and Big Ben.

> NARRATOR (VOICE-OVER)
> Only one person can stop them…

SFX: Big Ben STRIKES

> NARRATOR (VOICE-OVER)

…twelve-year-old local boy, Danny Brown.

EXTERIOR. DAY. A BRICK WALL.
Zoom in on DANNY'S frightened face.

EXTERIOR. DAY. AN ENGLISH FARM.
Shot of a barn seen from behind some flowers.

> MAN 1 (OFF SCREEN)

He must be around here somewhere. Check the barn.

SFX: FOOTSTEPS ON GRAVEL approach

Zoom in on barn door. A hand reaches out and slowly turns the door handle.

> NARRATOR (VOICE-OVER)

So far Danny Brown has slipped through VIPER's clutches…but now he faces a race against time.

SFX: The barn door CREAKS

SFX: a quick HEART BEAT

> NARRATOR (VOICE-OVER)

He'll need all his wits, speed and nerve.

EXTERIOR: A FIELD ON THE FARM.
Slow motion shot of DANNY running away.

> WOMAN 1 (VOICE-OVER)

Don't worry. The village is sealed off. There's no way out.

> NARRATOR (VOICE-OVER)

Can he escape and warn the government before it's too late…

EXTERIOR. DAY.
A snake moves on the ground, hissing.

> NARRATOR (VOICE-OVER)

…before the VIPER strikes? Watch out!

EXTERIOR. NIGHT.
Close-up on snake's face.

> NARRATOR (VOICE-OVER)

VIPER! Coming soon to a cinema near you.

Note: SFX means sound effects.